THE
BLUE MOUNTAINS

From any high-rise in Sydney a long blue range can be seen blocking the western horizon. Mts Tomah, Hay, Bell and Banks rise above the rest.

Two hundred years ago the community of British convicts, soldiers and settlers at Sydney also looked this way. For some, these blue ranges challenged their spirit of adventure; for others they were of scientific interest. But for all at the settlement, the Blue Mountains were a barrier. Convicts thought that China and freedom lay on the other side. Settlers and the military were blocked from acquiring land for stock and perhaps even gold mines for the opening.

In 1813 the Blue Mountains were finally crossed and the first "road" was built by William Cox a year later. The secret to the successful crossing was to avoid travelling the rivers, which always ended in waterfalls and incredible cliffs.

By May 1868 the railway had reached Mt Victoria. At the same time Sydney was becoming a most unhealthy town, with a foul water supply and outbreaks of typhoid, diphtheria, tuberculosis and even the plague. To escape the environment and the heat of summer, Sydney's wealthier citizens built country cottages and mansions on large blocks of land in the Blue Mountains. From the 1880s luxurious hotels were built at Katoomba, Medlow Bath, Jenolan Caves and Mt Victoria to give people access to magnificent scenery, "crisp and pure mountain air", the sparkling water and "Waratahs, Boronias and Orchids, which could be reaped by the armful". In the early days of tourism, the nature of the Blue Mountains was plundered.

Today, the mountains have been restored and most lie within the national park. Early walking tracks, built with inspired hard work and imagination, which lead to lookouts, waterfalls and into the forested depths of Grose Gorge and Jamison Valley, are once again serviceable. However, no matter how many structures are provided, the great golden cliffs, the blue deeps, forested valleys and the ringing, echoing calls of lyrebirds and Mountain Currawongs will remain the real attraction. Cars can take us to the edge of all this, but only by exercising our legs and imbibing the crisp, heady air can we really enter Blue Mountain majesty.

Steve Parish
PUBLISHING

Above, clockwise from left: *The golden crags of Hanging Rock near Govetts Leap, Blackheath; layers of sandstone and shale; Kanangra Creek plunging into the Thurat Deeps; escarpment near Govetts Leap.*

CLIFFS AND VALLEYS

About 200 million years ago a vast shining bay was here. Around Bathurst and down Goulburn way were high mountains being worn down by rain and wind. Very large rivers poured into this bay from the mountains and carried sand, mud and pebbles until sedimentary beds were kilometres deep. Then, very slowly, the bed of the sea began to rise like a fantastic whale, shedding the water from its back. The sand had become layers of sandstone, and the mud shale.

There has been plenty of time for new rivers—the Grose, the Warragamba, Cox and Kowmung—to carry out their work in carving out magnificent valleys, gorges and canyons. Layers of shale are the weaknesses below the massive sandstones. As they rot out, the undermined sandstones collapse leaving 200-metre, glorious pink and golden walls. Silvery waterfalls drop from the high valleys and hanging swamps into rainforest depths.

Top: *Boars Head with Mt Solitary across the Jamison Valley.* **Above:** *Kanangra Walls and the walking track to Mt Cloudmaker.*

NOVEL WAYS TO SEE MOUNTAINS

Katoomba originally had a small coalmine and a timber industry. The coal lay in a narrow seam below the cliffs. A very steep set of tracks was laid so trucks of coal could be winched up to the roadway. Today, however, it is visitors who take this easy but thrilling way down to the walking tracks below the cliffs. These tracks, which run to Mt Solitary, The Castle, Landslide and Giants Stairway, frequently pass through ferny tunnels and rainforest groves by cascading creeks.

Thrill-seekers can also reach the old coalmines and walking tracks by riding 545 metres down into the valley on the Scenic Flyway.

For those wishing to gain an aerial view of the valley treetops and spectacular views of the clifflines and Three Sisters, particularly in late afternoon, the Scenic Skyway cable car is a grand way to do it.

Top: *The mountains are best seen in all their glory by riding the Scenic Flyway.*
Above: *Scenic Railway taking visitors to the valley floor.*

Above: *The Scenic Skyway cable car, 300 metres above the head of Kedumba River.*

Once the railway from Sydney reached Katoomba in the 1860s the mountains were easily accessible. Hiking became the favourite activity along tens of kilometres of superbly made tracks. Some of the special trains became famous—the "Fish" and the "Chips" were two.

After work on Fridays the trains to the mountains were packed with hikers, picnickers, bushwalkers and cyclists. Service cars (or charabancs as they were once called) picked walkers up from Mt Victoria and Lithgow to drop them at Jenolan and Kanangra for stunning bushwalks back to Katoomba.

Today, horseback riding and travel by mountain bike and canoe are other popular ways to see the Blue Mountains.

Left: *A minaret stalactite formation, Jenolan Caves, built by the slow deposit of calcite from millions of drops of water.*
Above: *A quaint place to stay while exploring the nearby wonders—Caves House, Jenolan Caves.*

Above: *From Kings Tableland across the great ravine of Jamison Valley to Katoomba.* **Below:** *Echo Point to the Three Sisters and Mt Solitary.*

A WORLD-CLASS VIEW

The road and railway to Katoomba from Emu Plains climbs in three great steps to over 1100 metres. To stand anywhere along that remarkable curving rim from Kings Tableland to Narrow Neck or to gaze into the vast hollow of the Grose River from Govetts Leap or Evans Lookout is to stand on the edge of wilderness. The floors of the valleys lie over 1000 metres below.

Charles Darwin on his momentous world journey commented that "this kind of view was to me quite novel, and extremely magnificent". He went on to describe the scene:

If we imagine a winding harbour, with its deep water surrounded by bold cliff-like shores, laid dry, and a forest sprung up on its sandy bottom we should then have the appearance and structure here exhibited.

No doubt the deep blues and shadowy purples suggested the marine comparison.

A group of French scientists compared nightfall over the mountains with that over South American forests, except that: "here all was silent, we dared not break that religious calm, which seemed to invite meditation."

Sometimes silent, occasionally misty and mysterious, most frequently these golden clifflines are lit dramatically by the brass of sunrise. But always international visitors are bewitched by the blue shadow of distances beneath the rim of gold.

Above: *Leura and Katoomba, with Kanangra Walls on the horizon.*

OF FERNY GLADES AND QUIET FORESTS

Sandstone produces a poor soil, but here in the Blue Mountains rifts opened, pouring lava across many places. Today only a little remains, protecting the crowns of Mts Wilson, Bell, Tomah, Banks and Hay. This weathering basalt rock produced pockets of fertile soil when it washed into the glens and valleys. In these wet and fertile places, as well as on soils from the shales, a magic green world of rainforest is nourished. These are the shadowed, silent places where our footfall is muffled by fallen leaves redolent of fungus. Out to one side, clear water rushes over boulders and slides beneath mossy logs. This too is almost a world on its own, filling a tunnel beneath the king ferns and the tree fern *Dicksonia antarctica*. So many of the plants of these cool, wet ecosystems had their ancestry in the cool forests of the ancient supercontinent called Gondwana.

Today, these glens are the summer refuges for birds, wallabies, wombats and visiting humans.

Three places close to Katoomba stand out—Blackheath Glen on the road to Megalong Valley; the Grand Canyon walk from the Evans Lookout road; the walks within Katoomba Creek and about the lower end of the Scenic Railway. Winter walking provides the added glory of a lyrebird accompaniment.

Top: *The Eastern Grey Kangaroo, alert and watching.*

Above: *Temperate rainforest of the Blue Mountains, featuring lillypilly and coachwood.*
Below: *Fern-lined creeks in Blackheath Glen rainforest.*

Today, thousands of people cross the Blue Mountains by car, express train, and by jet at 5000 or more metres. It wasn't always like that:

Here we pause, surveying the wild abyss; pondering our voyage! Before us lay the trackless desert, in awful silence. . .save that a melancholy crow flew croaking overhead, or a kangaroo was seen to bound at a distance, the picture of solitude was complete and undisturbed.

So wrote Captain Tench in 1790. The Nepean River was the frontier. Now, one can leave the carpark at Kanangra Walls or even at Evans Lookout and, from the cliff edge, experience the same feeling. Those wild escarpments are still the frontier to nature, thanks to the National Park status for most of this vast mountain area. Apart from the flooding of Burragorang Valley and Cox River by the giant Warragamba Dam (nine times the volume of Sydney Harbour) for Sydney's water supply, the wilderness is almost intact.

Amazingly, the first road was built with convict labour by William Cox in one year, between 1814 and 1815. Soon the trickle of people using the road became a flood, particularly when gold discoveries at Bathurst received official recognition in 1851. One can imagine the hordes of immigrants with barrows, the stage coaches, gold escorts and bullock wagons stirring the road to dust and mud. What a ferment! The courthouse at Hartley, designed by Colonial Architect, Mortimer Lewis and opened in 1837, saw much use during this time.

Clockwise from top left: *The Hydro-Majestic at Medlow Bath; Imperial Hotel, Mount Victoria; The Norman Lindsay studio, Springwood; "Leuralla", a beautifully preserved home that houses the NSW Toy and Railway Museum and the Dr H V Evatt Memorial Museum.*

Above: *The Great Zig Zag, Mt Victoria.* **Following pages:** *Three Sisters, focal point of the Blue Mountains.*

WHY THREE SISTERS?

Once long ago in the mountains there was a clever old man called Tyawan who had three daughters: Meenhi, Wimlah and Gunnedoo. Old Tyawan could imitate the bush creatures and with the aid of a magic shinbone could turn himself into a lyrebird. When Tyawan went hunting in the valley, he told his daughters to stay on the cliff top, safe from the powerful spirit, Bunyip, which lived in a waterhole deep in the valley.

One day, Meenhi knocked a rock over the cliff and it started a landslide. The terrible Bunyip awoke, saw the girls clinging together on the cliff top and charged towards them. Old Tyawan could not reach the scene in time, so used his magic shinbone to change his daughters into rocks so the Bunyip could not harm them.

Then the Bunyip chased old Tyawan, who deceived him by imitating other creatures and at last changed himself into a lyrebird, dropping his magic shinbone as his hands became wings.

The Bunyip went back into his waterhole and went to sleep again. To this day, old Tyawan the Lyrebird scratches through the leaves trying to find his magic shinbone. And until he finds it, Tyawan will remain a lyrebird and his three daughters will remain the stony Three Sisters, safe on their cliff top.

Left and above: *The Three Sisters look out over Jamison Valley from Cliff Drive, Katoomba Falls.*
Above right: *Superb Lyrebird in display singing for the female.*

Left to right: *Leaves touched by the magic of autumn begin their splendid run down through golds and reds, until they drop to soften the ground with a fiery carpet; Gang Gang Cockatoo.*

THE MOSAIC OF AUTUMN

While discovering areas along the western railway, escapees from degraded, disease-ridden 19th-century Sydney found themselves welcomed by a climate reminiscent of the "old country", England. The Blue Mountains quickly became a favoured retreat for brisk walks and recreation, as well as providing a chance to enjoy the magnificent scenery.

In time, lush formal gardens of exotic flowering plants were laid out around mansions, grand hotels and cottages—particularly at Katoomba, Blackheath, and Leura and by the Lindsays at Springwood. Avenues of beeches, oaks, elms, walnuts, maples, liquid ambers, camellias and magnolias were planted. Dark pines and cypresses added stunning variations in colour, form and texture. Roses, fuschias, bluebells and snowdrops completed a nostalgic portrait of the English garden in all its glory.

Autumn is the perfect season for exploring the Blue Mountains, providing a wonderful setting for all kinds of recreational activity: bushwalking, mountaineering, horse riding, fishing, or just the simple pleasures of a family picnic.

Above and below: *Mt Wilson, where the deep green shaded avenues of summer have waned with the first frosts catching the fires of autumn.*

ON MISTY MORNINGS

There are certain mornings when, to look out from Echo Point, Govetts Leap or from anywhere along the rocky rim, it feels as if you are among a massive fleet of rocky ships floating on an ocean of cloud. From June to August, out of the valley mist, the muffled but still clear notes of the lyrebird reach out to you. A crimson shrieking flash marks the wave-like flight of parrots as they career from cliff-top gums. From a sunny branch, the bell-like tones of a solitary Australian King-Parrot seek out the green female somewhere below in the misted tree-fern country.

While many Blue Mountain townsfolk are still to brave the quiet chill of morning, others have already chased their panting, steaming breath to board the "Fish" for Sydney workplaces, which gives time to read the news before mixing it with city crowds.

Above: *Mist shrouding the valleys, caressing the jagged cliff edges.*

Top: *Lyrebird habitat, Mt Victoria.* **Above:** *The green tips of trees peek through the enveloping mist.*
Below, left to right: *Sulphur-crested Cockatoos; the Crimson Rosella known locally as the Blue Mountain Parrot.*

PERCHED WHERE EAGLES FLY

Surveyor Evans followed Blaxland, Wentworth and Lawson (1813) who laid out the route across the Blue Mountains. Cox directed the roadwork, which made way for the establishment of a line of towns that today, like steps in a giant ladder, span the mountains from Glenbrook to Mt Victoria. The lower towns lead towards six further towns seemingly perched on the edge of space—Wentworth Falls, Leura, Katoomba, Medlow Bath, Blackheath and Mt Victoria.

Nearby are 200–300 metre precipices, massive sandstone walls dropping sheer onto forested slopes. But the first grand hollows or gorges (and whatever else bushwalkers are wont to call these challenging places) are those out from Jenolan and Kanangra Walls. The ridge-tops ascending to the vast hump of Mt Cloudmaker go by the comical names of Rick, Rack, Roar and Rumble. From these heights it is possible to look down on the soaring Wedge-tailed Eagles and watch Peregrines swoop on unwary cockatoos.

Left: *Mt Cloudmaker in the Kanangra–Boyd area.*
Top and above left: *Views of Katoomba.* **Above right:** *Aerial view of Blackheath, a picturesque Blue Mountains town.*

FOREST DISCOVERIES

It was over 100 years ago that people began to build holiday houses and hotels along the railway. They found ways into the narrow gullies and breaks in the cliffs and, from these, into the valleys of the rivers. For many, the misty mountains and deep forested gullies and valleys were reminiscent of Scotland.

So glens were named Blackheath Glen and Centennial Glen. The early settlers found them to be full of moss-encrusted boulders, king ferns and tree ferns. Shiny, dark-green leaved lillypillies rose from the damp mulch-filled soils throwing out sprays of soft-pink fruit, to the delight of King-Parrots. Leathery, pale-grey, lichen-encrusted trunks of coachwoods, sisters of the Christmas bush, carried magnificent heads of pale flowers which became reddish, flower-like fruit when conditions were right. There was always the rich mouldy smell of rotting leaves, within which lived tiny brown amphipods, worms and insects, prized food of the lyrebird. In the cold, sparkling creek waters splendid red and black yabbies slowly strutted among mosaics of fallen leaves.

Clockwise from top: *Cool, ferny rainforest glens are tucked in near the cliffs and waterfalls; ferns flourish in the moist environment; Australian King-Parrot.*

Clockwise from top: *Castle Head and Mt Solitary from The Landslide—all around is woodland; Common Wombat; Swamp Wallaby.*

WOODLAND ENCOUNTERS

Sandstone breaks down to sand that is unable to provide much plant food or hold water for long on the slopes. Here the trees are shorter and spread further apart with many shrubs and grasses.

These woodlands smell strongly of eucalyptus and other spicy odours. It is the tiny droplets of oil given off by the trees that filter the light and make the mountains blue.

If you walk the woodland tracks carefully and with little noise, it is possible to meet many shy animals. There are three macropods—the large, soft-furred Eastern Grey and the Red-necked Wallaby in the shrubby understory; and then the sooty-coloured, very timid Swamp Wallaby, usually heard but not seen. The Common Wombat, too, lives in large burrows in the woodlands of the mountains. A variety of dragon and skink lizard species usually scurry out of your path. But listen closely to the bird calls, particularly the Rufous Whistler's ringing "ee-chong" and the melodious Grey Shrike-thrush—it will follow for kilometres if one imitates its call.

FALLING WATER

Diamond Falls is off the side of Narrow Neck and, like Bridal Veil Falls at Govetts Leap, a thin stream of sparkling water wanders ever so slowly over the edge. From there it responds to every mood, every eddy in the wind. It is like a living stream: dropping, wandering, sometimes even defying gravity by drifting upwards. Eventually, it spatters on the black shining rocks below.

As a bushwalker years ago, I camped in mid-winter just above Diamond Falls with a howling south-wester blowing. Stars were sharp and clear in the blackness and from time to time a shower from the reversed waterfall sprayed down like icy needles. By morning the wind had died and, by daylight in the bitter chill, all of the surrounding vegetation, the bright green mallee leaves, banksias, the red and white native fuschias and the delicate pink dogroses were shining, glassy images. The early sun played games with bewitching, refracting light. Presently, in the warming sun, the bush began to shake off its icy coat. First the red gum tips came to life while the larger green leaf surfaces slipped their panes of ice with tiny clinking sounds. The air stirred and the whole bush shook itself free in a constellation of sparkling stars. From our perch on the edge of the cliff muffled waves of spattering sound came and went just like the cool dampness forming beads on our hair.

Each of the many waterfalls has its special time of day and its moods. All of them are gossamer steps and stairs to paradise.

Left: *The delicate tracery of Wentworth Falls.*
Above: *Cascading waters of Beauchamp Falls run over steep cliff edges.*

THE MAGNIFICENT GUM TREE

It has been said that only when one appreciates the beauty of the gum tree has one become truly Australian. Viewed through the eyes of 19th-century English naturalist, Charles Darwin, these trees "with their scanty colour-less foliage and dead bark hanging from their trunks appeared lifeless, dreary and monotonous". Monotonous or not, the eucalypt, 170 years later, is now the most widely planted tree in the world.

For Australian wildlife, the old gum tree is "nature's boarding house". Its hollow branches are homes for parrots and cockatoos, possums and those remarkable gliders, the phalangers—Sugar Glider, Yellow-bellied Glider, Greater Glider and sometimes even the tiny mouse-like Feathertail Glider.

Honey-laden flowers provide food for possums and gliders as do leaves of some gums for the Koala. Some of the gliders have found how to break into the tree's sap supply by chewing through the bark. Termites consume the tree's wood and some types build large nests up in the tree while others live in the ground. Kookaburras tunnel their nests into the treetop termite homes, thereby having a ready-made food supply for their chicks. Short-beaked Echidnas, Australia's only echidna species, rip apart the ground nests and lap up the streaming termites.

Above: *Ribbon gums stand tall and strong among the abundance of flora.*

Above: *Rocky outcrops softened with eucalypts.*
Below, clockwise from top left: *Friendly residents: Crimson Rosella, Echidna, Sugar Glider; Kookaburra.*

AT DAY'S END

Helmeted climbers abseil from the middle Sister as the shadows behind them deepen from powder blue to royal purple. The air has the first puffs of chill. Smoke rises from the yellow clearings at Kedumba to settle as a layer. Above, the chalky yellow cliffs are catching the last glow of the setting sun.

Beyond, east towards Sydney, model cumulus are rolling upwards, tops to be whipped into classic anvil heads, a study in golden fleece.

Across the mountain towns, the vast walls of Mt Banks are also alight. The amphitheatre of Grose Gorge is engulfed in cobalt touched with purple. The heads of just a few of the monumental blue gums are gilt with the rays of the fading sun.

The bell-like notes of a currawong, planing in a looping glide far below, echo hauntingly from cliff to cliff. Then all is quiet as shadows climb to the summit of Mt Banks. Evening is falling—there is the sensation of chill. Tomorrow will be another fine day.

Above: *The Three Sisters, aglow and majestic.*

Above: *Blue Mountains magic at sunset.*
Below, left to right: *A Mountain Brushtail Possum foraging at night; perched in the treetops preparing for take off, the Greater Glider.*